COPYRIGHT © 2020 HAPPY ARTS COLORING

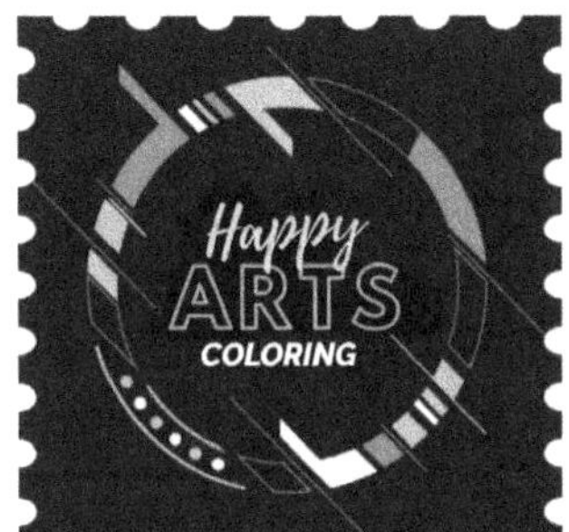

Walk in the Village

fantasy coloring books for adults

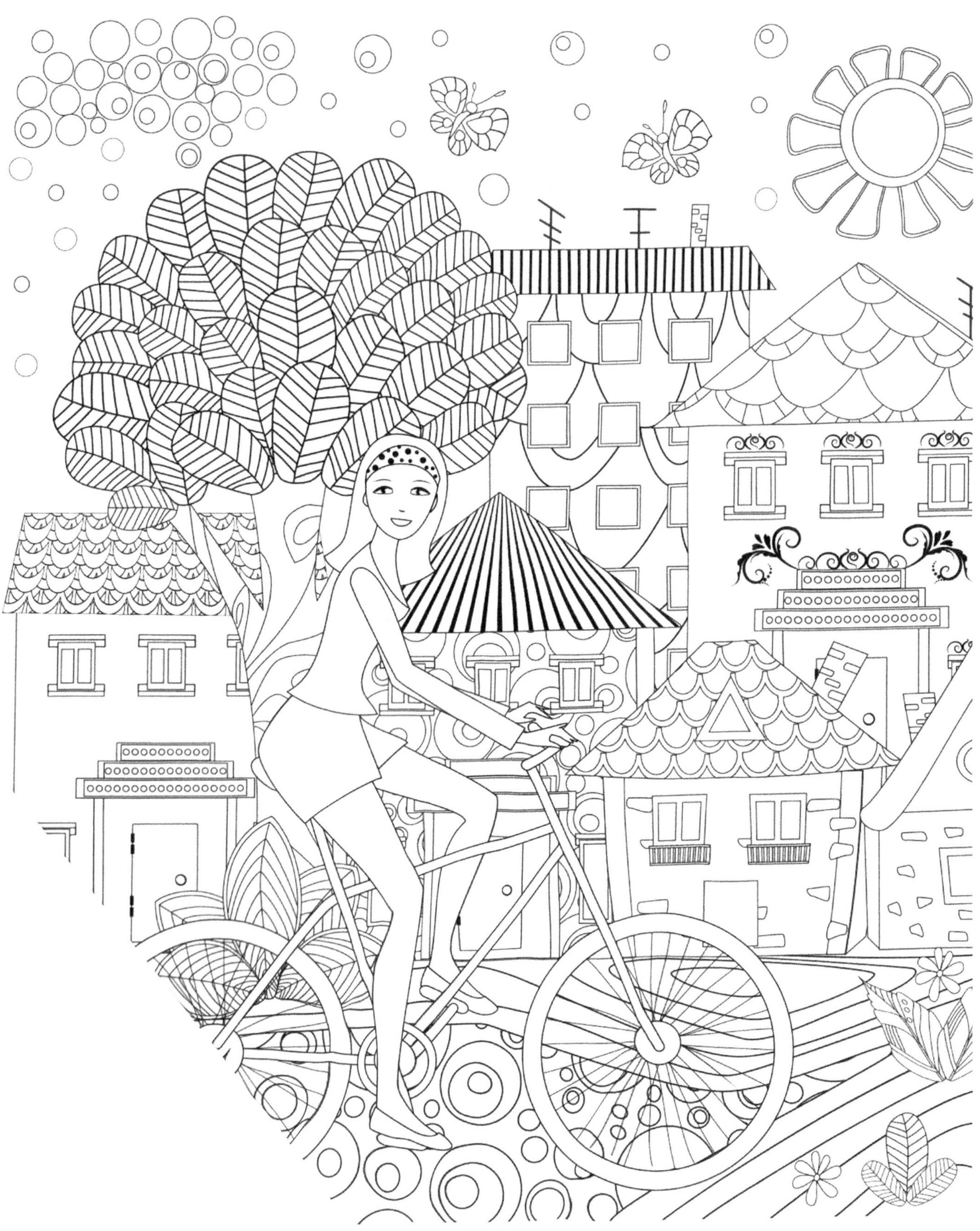

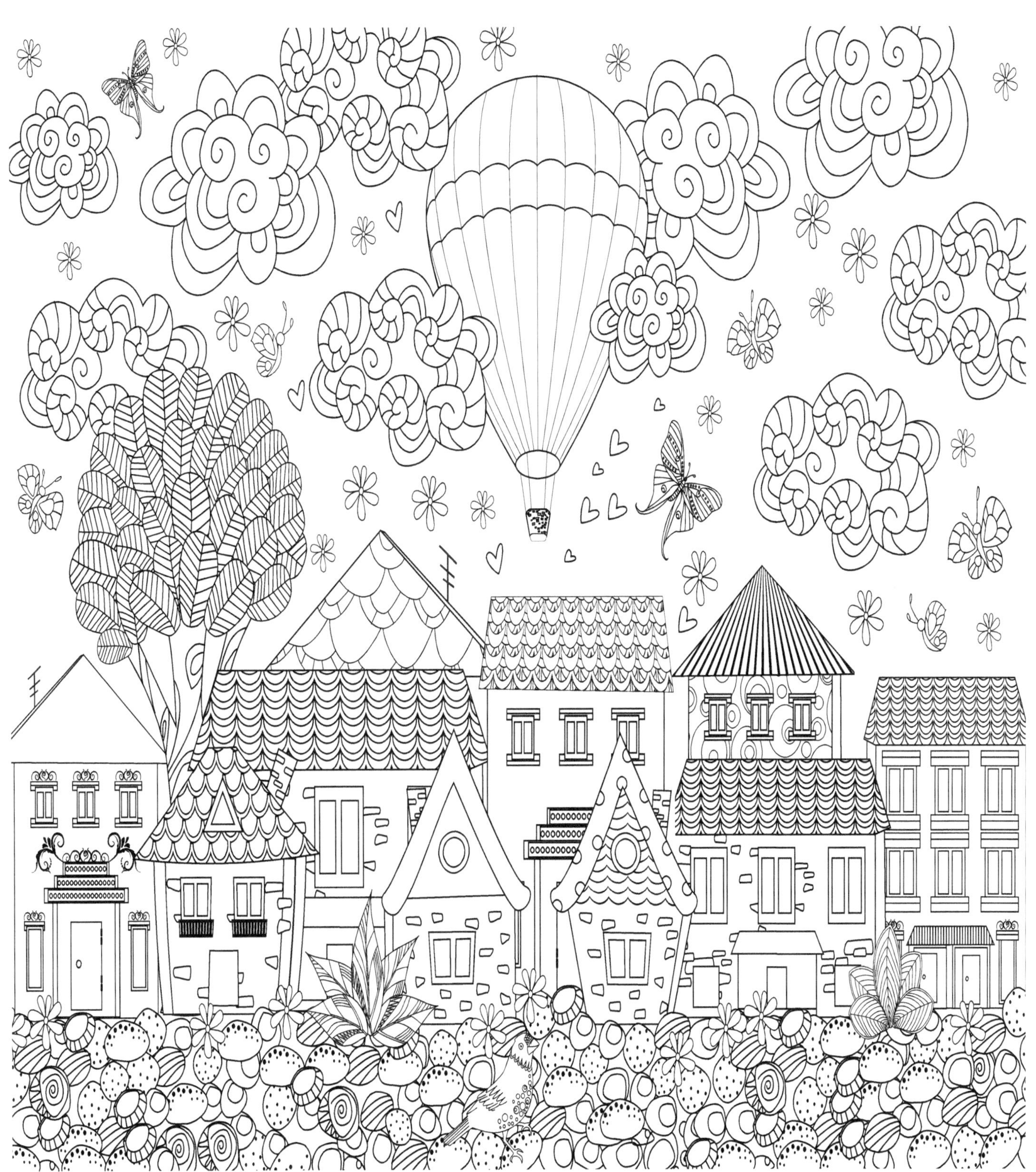

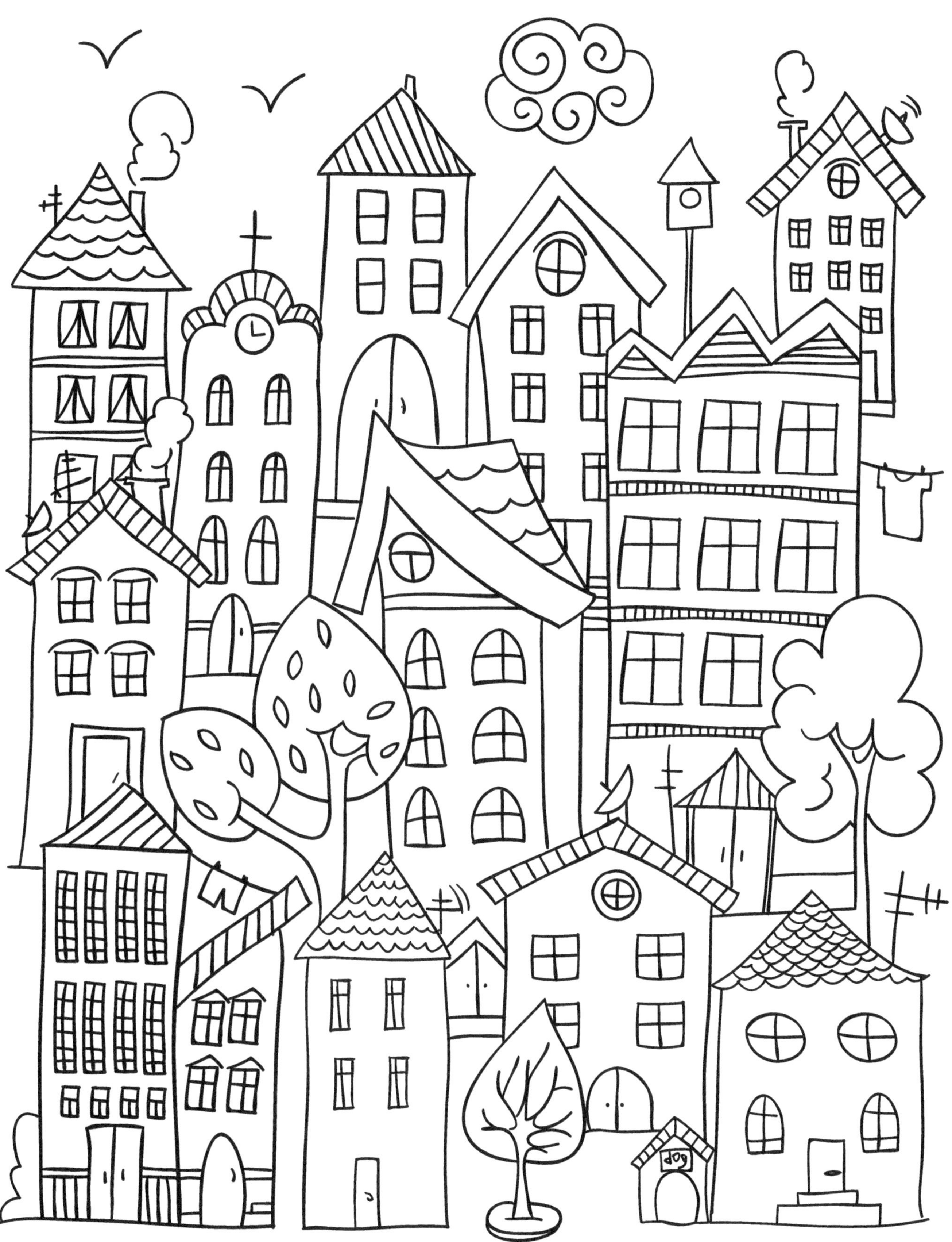

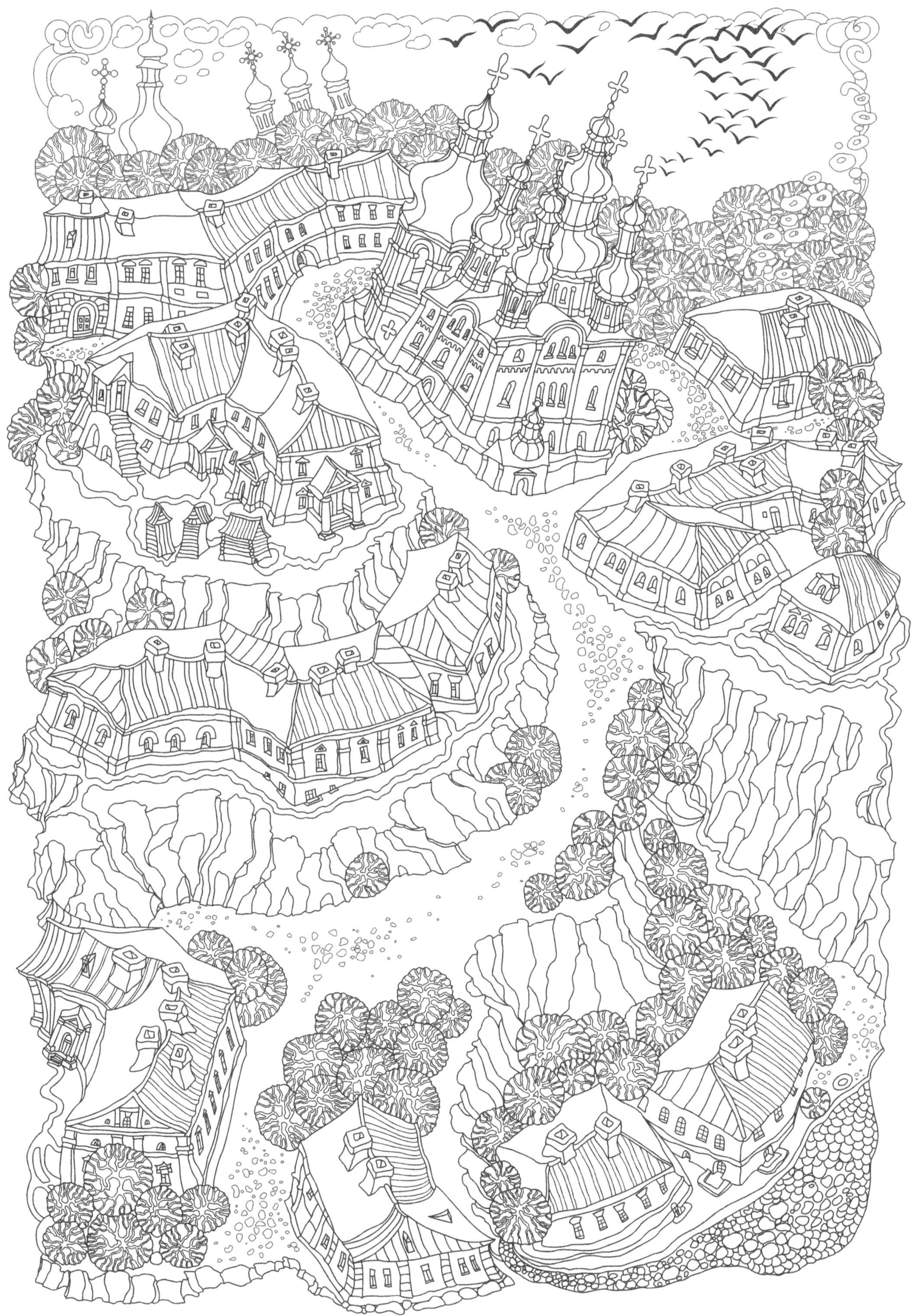

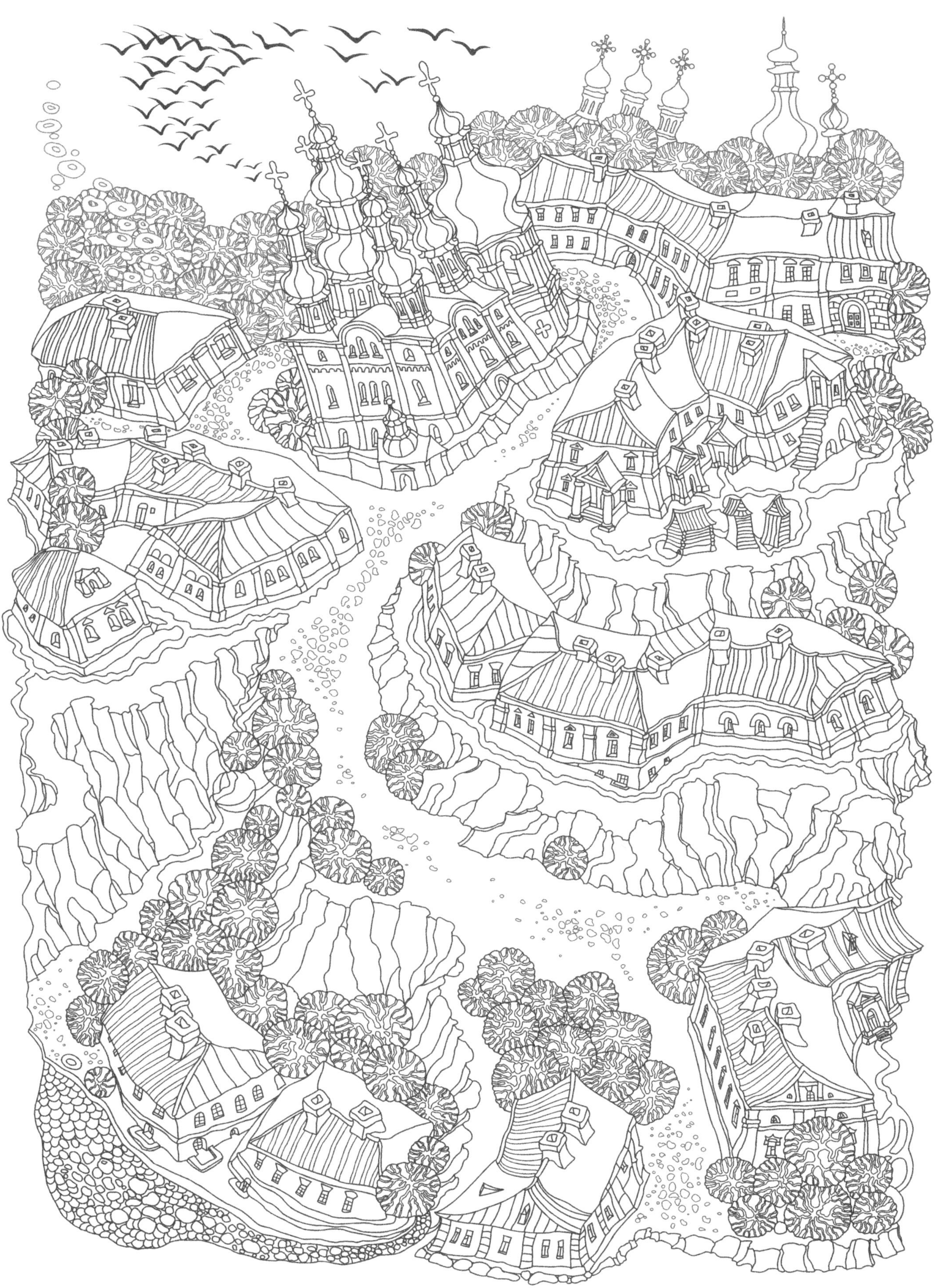

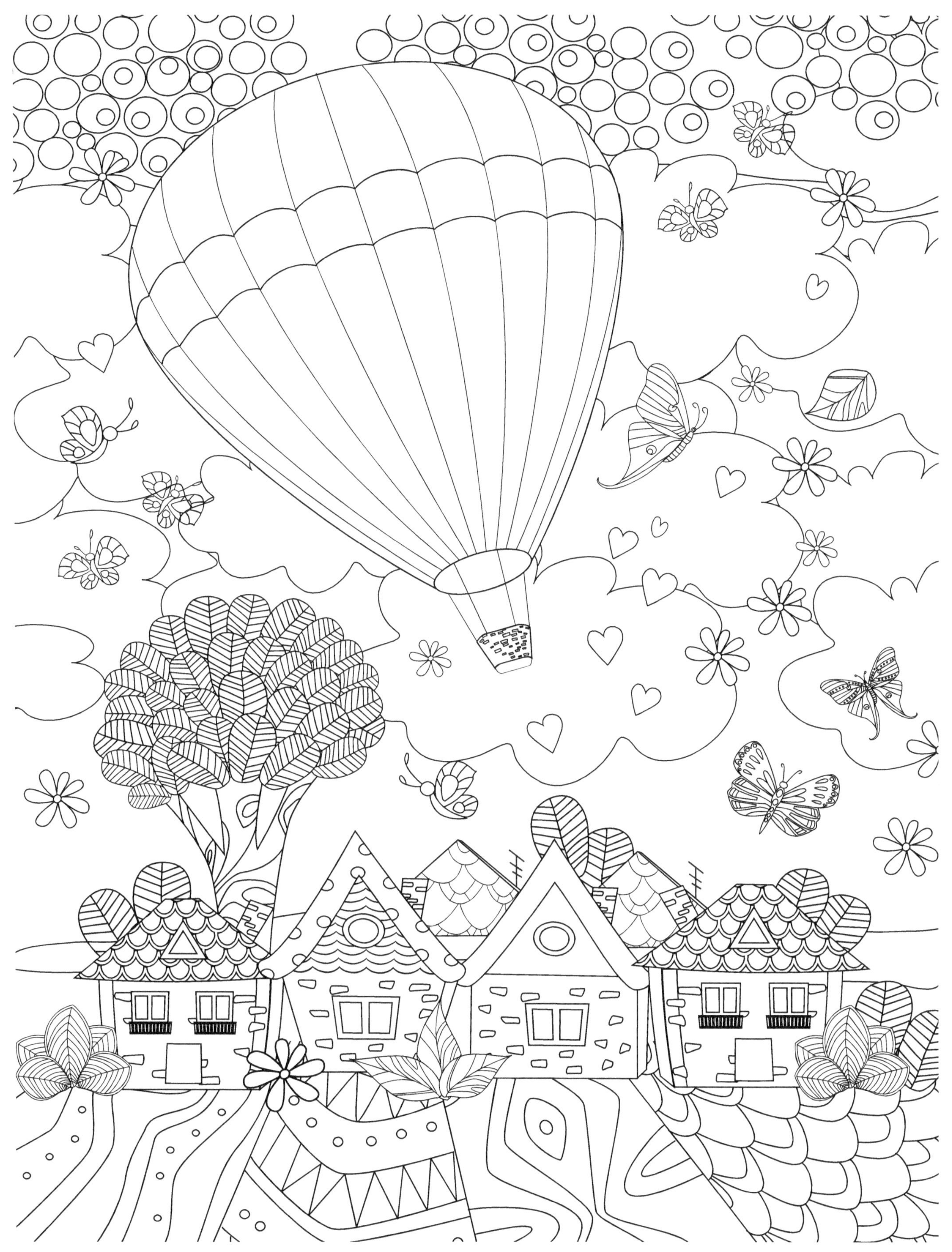

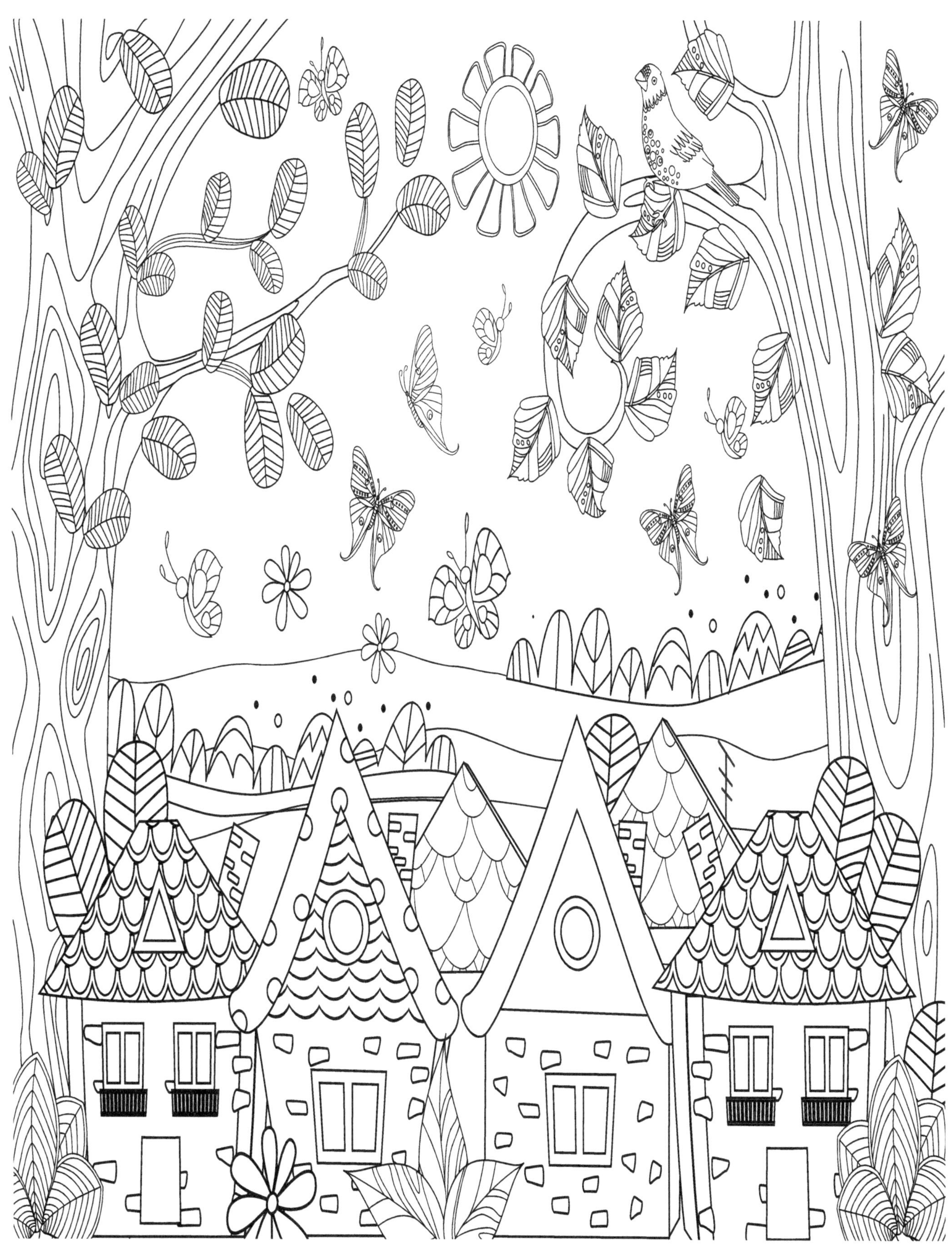

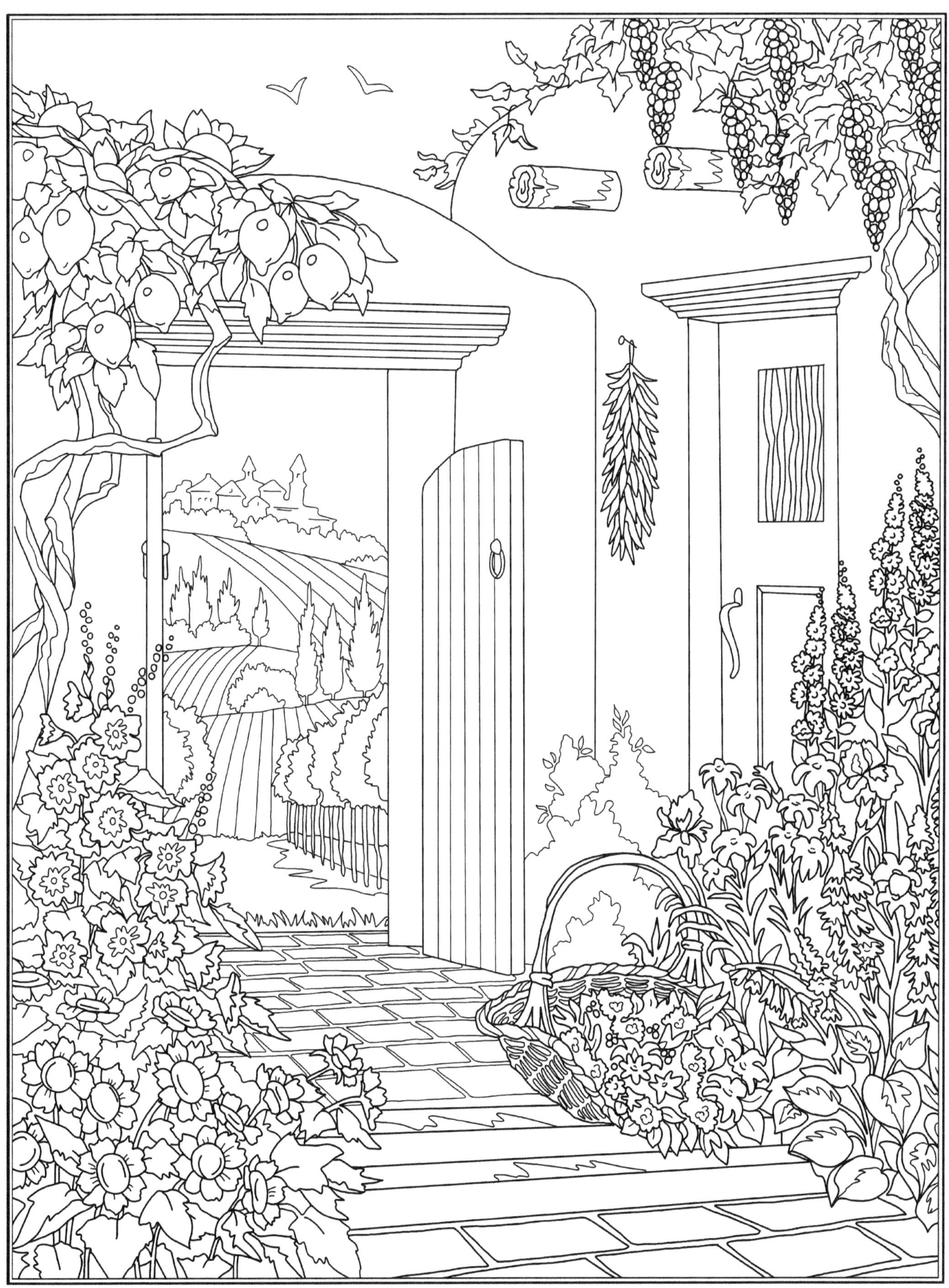

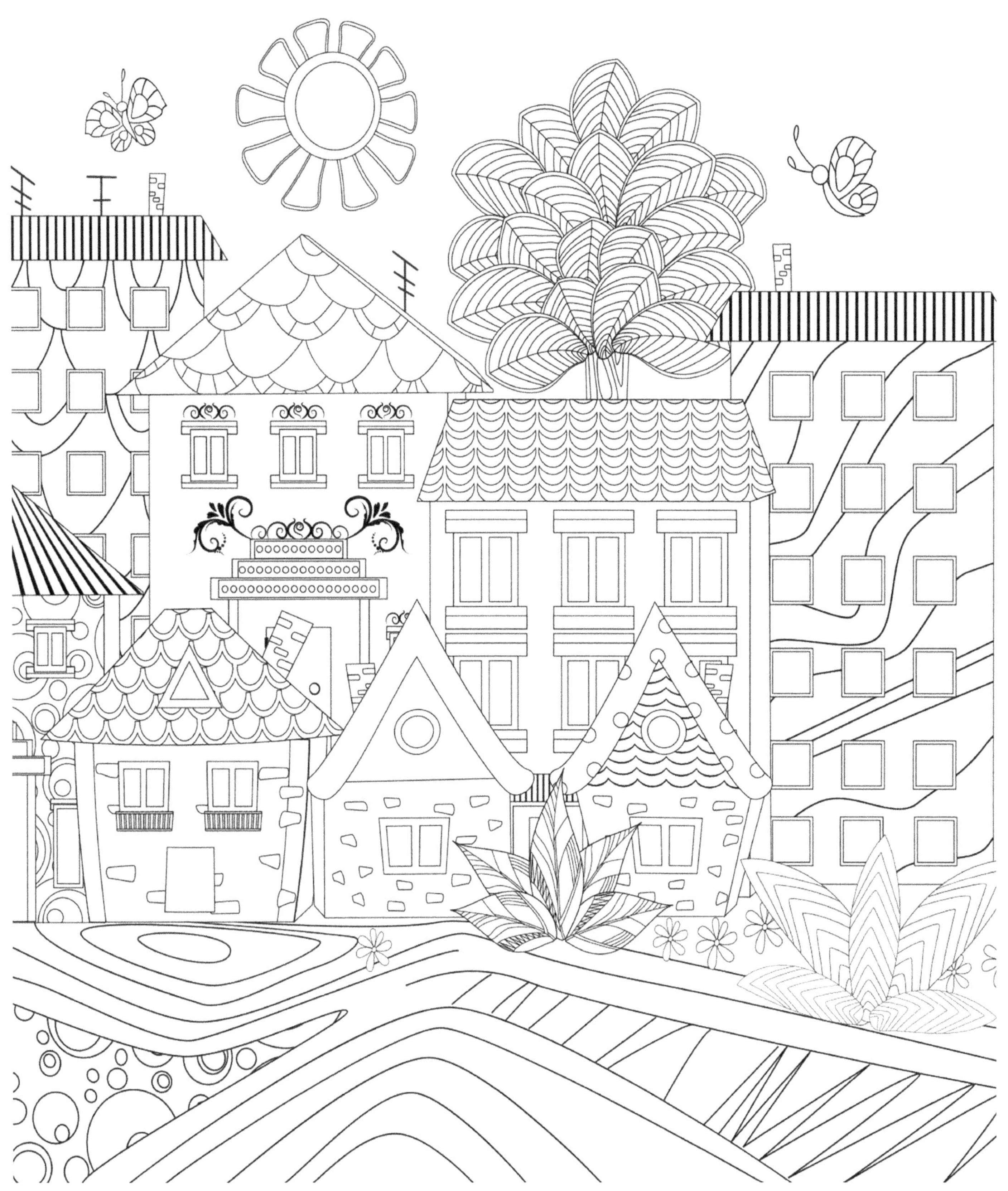

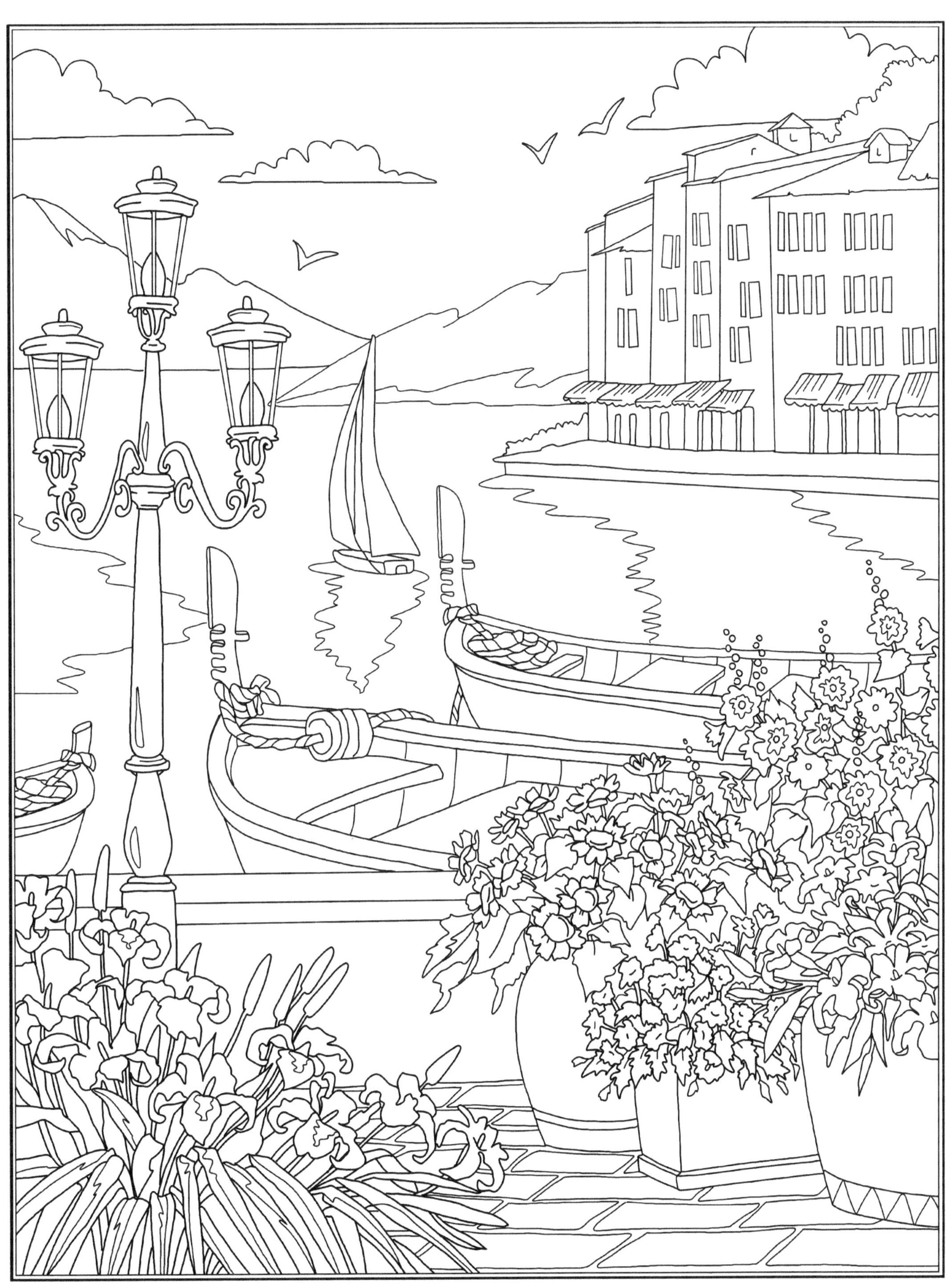

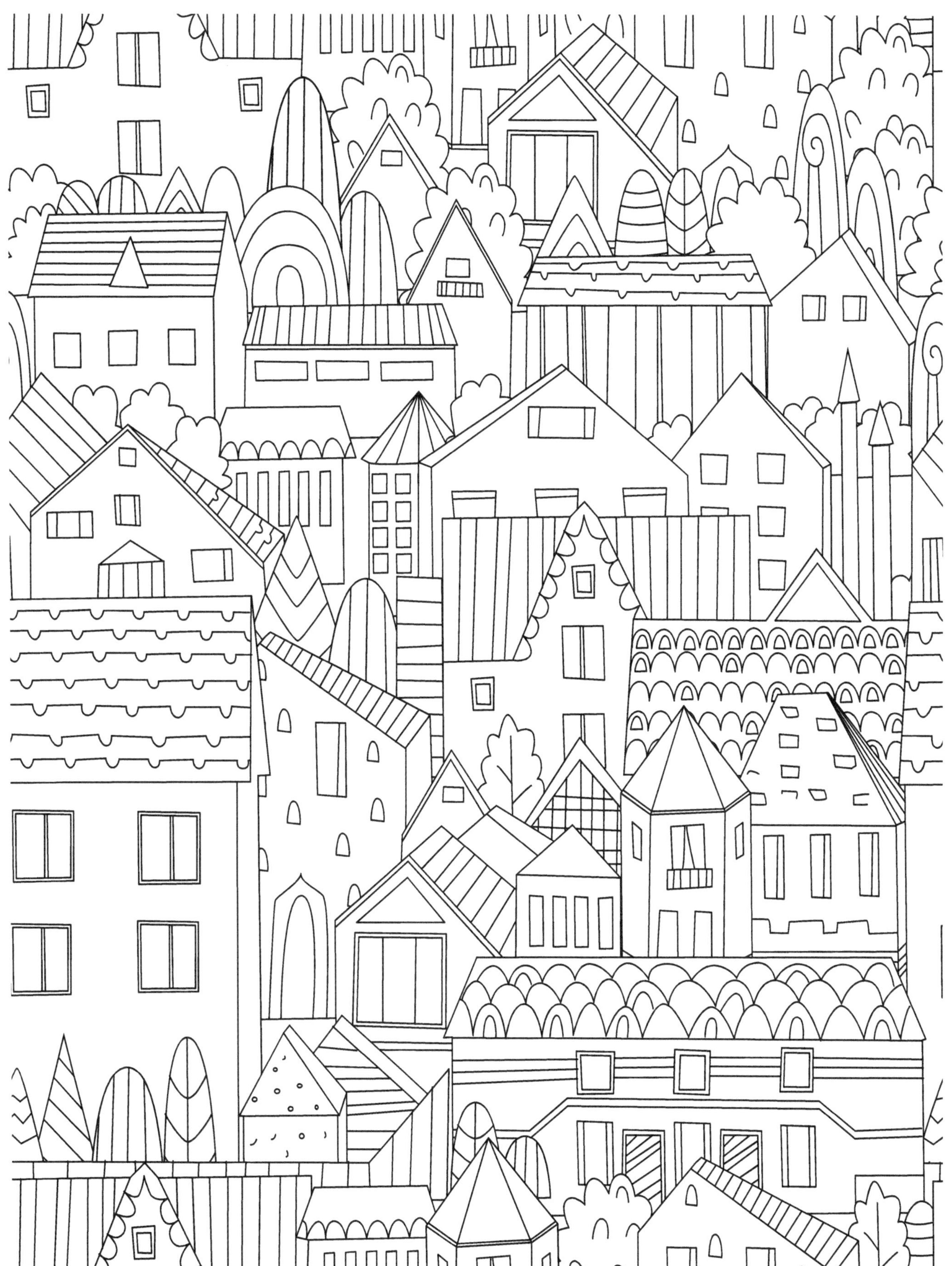

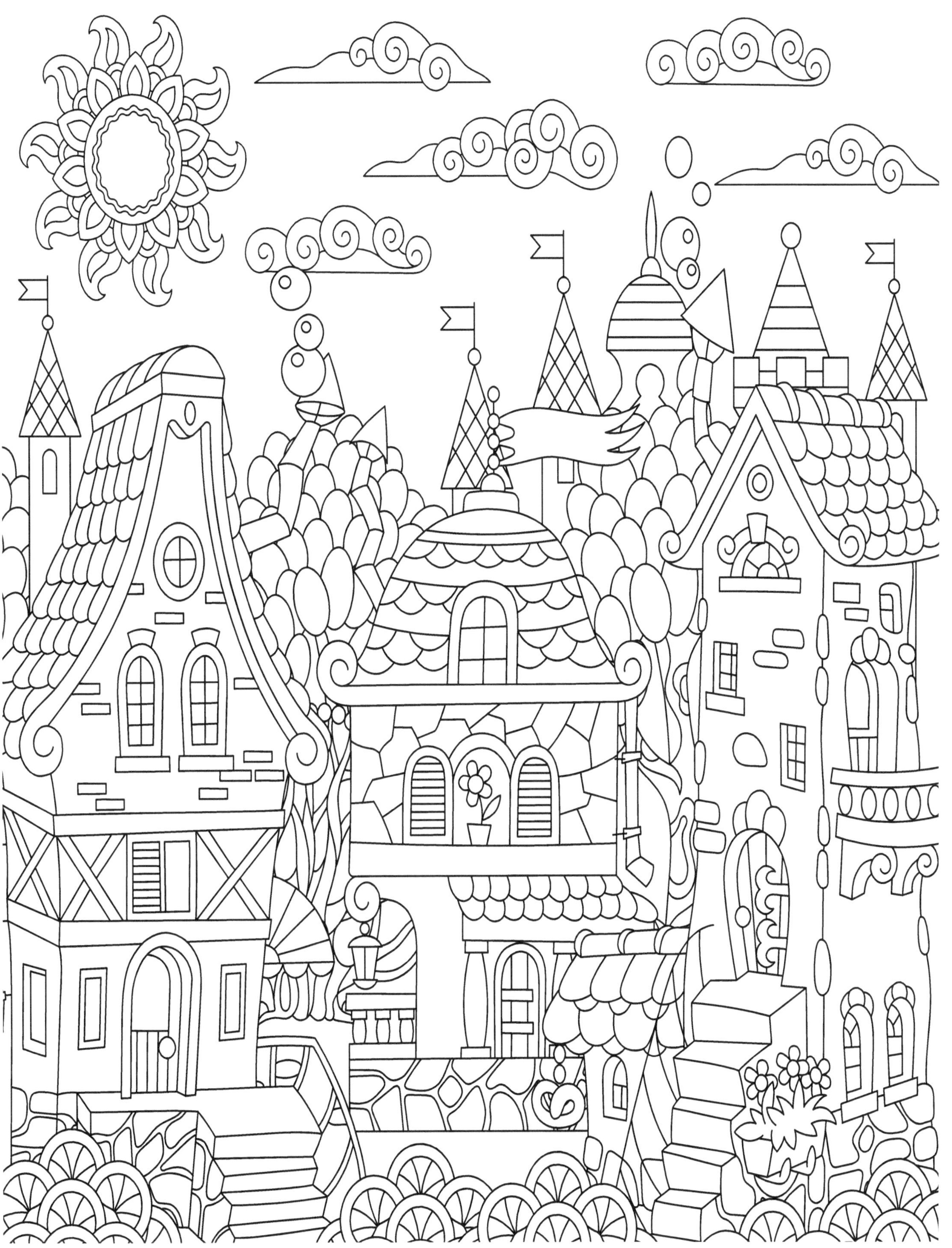

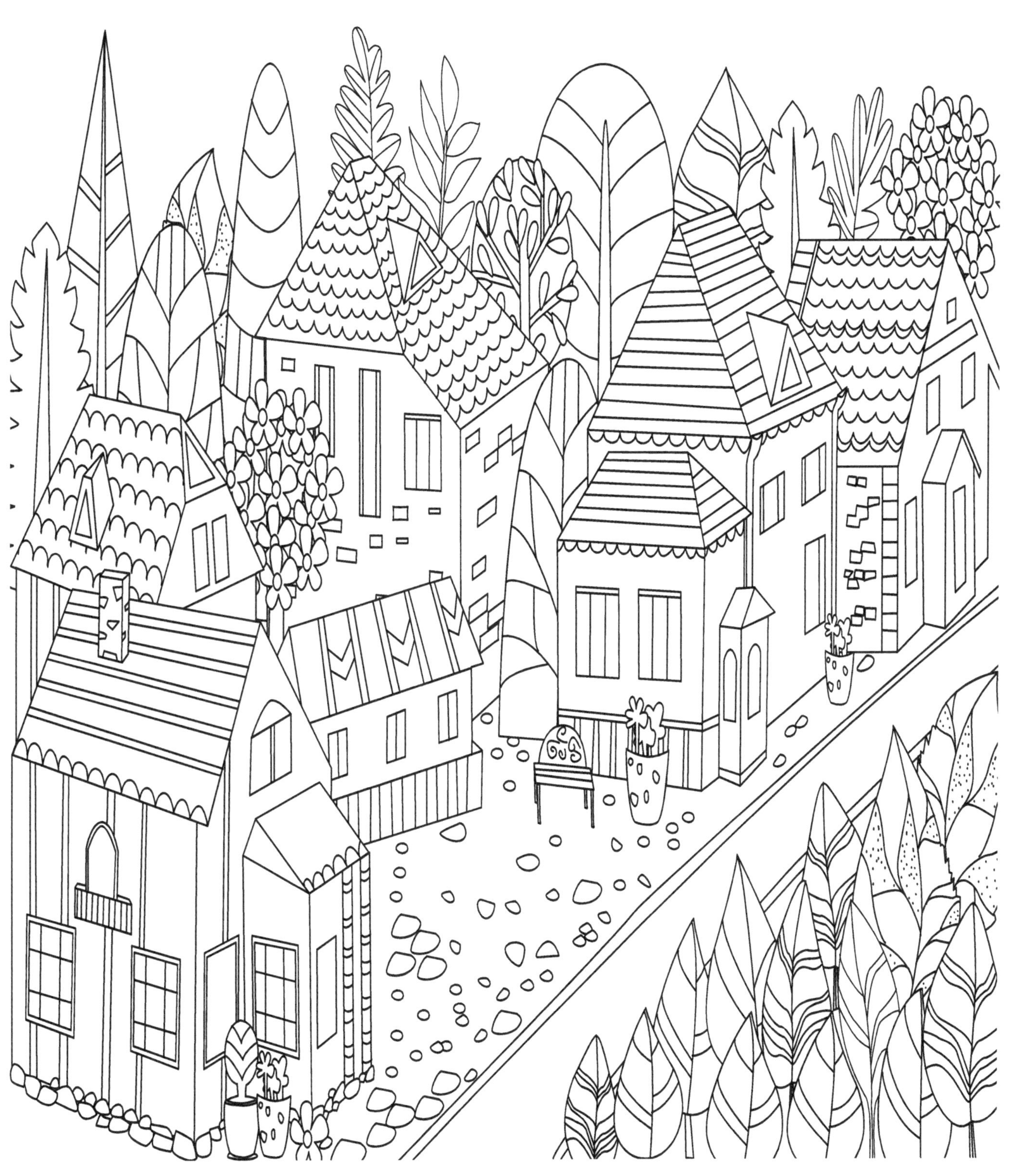

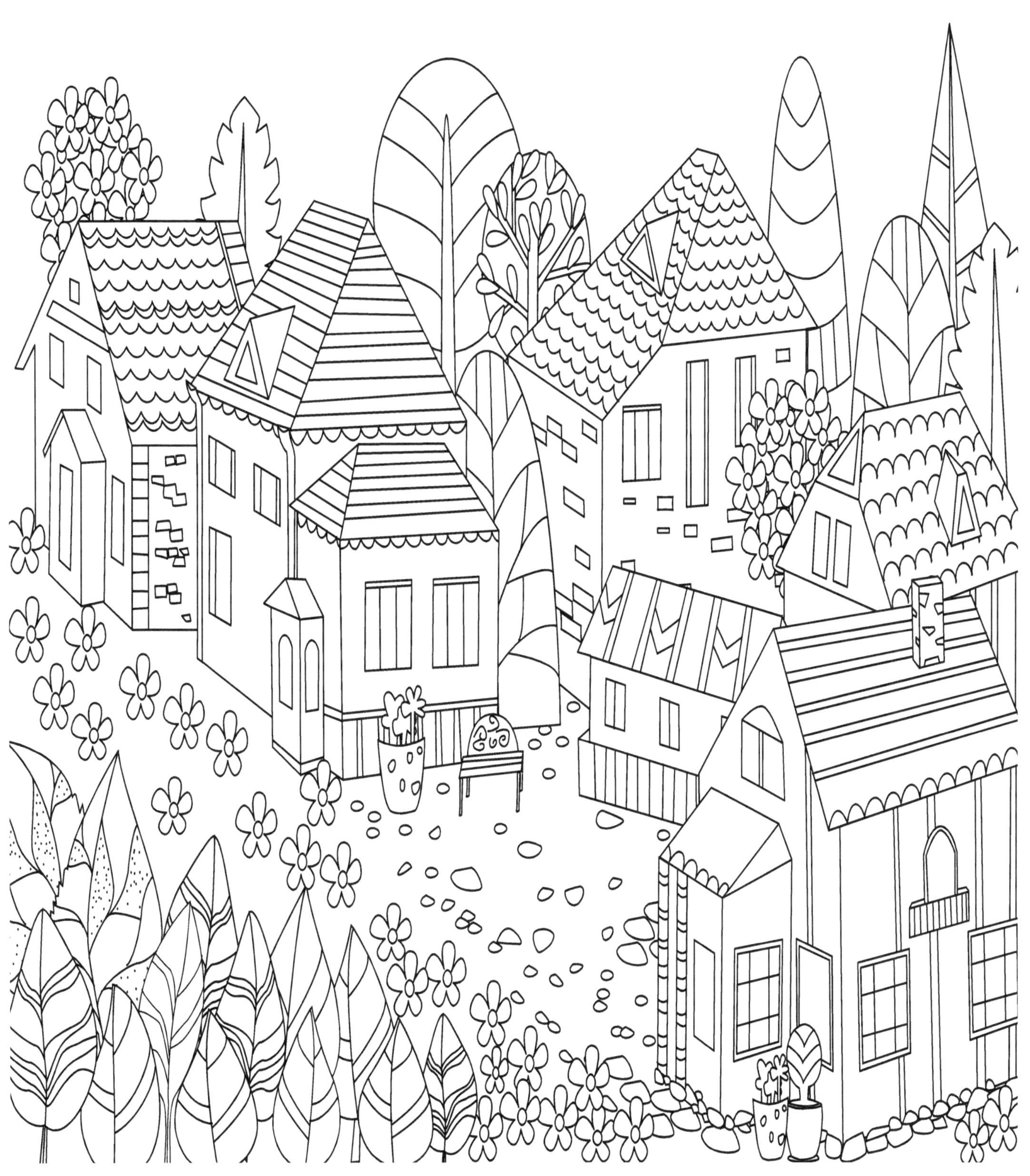

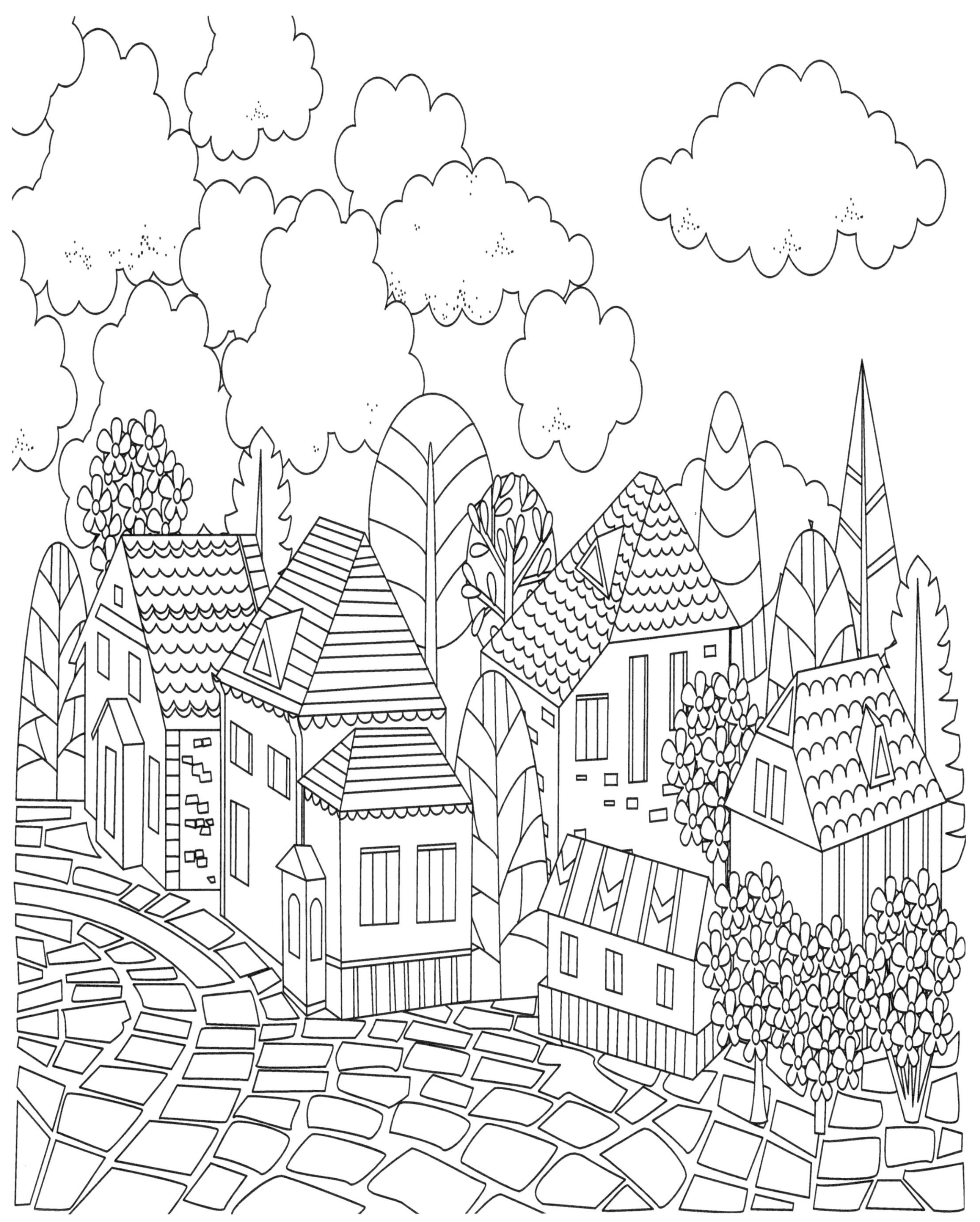

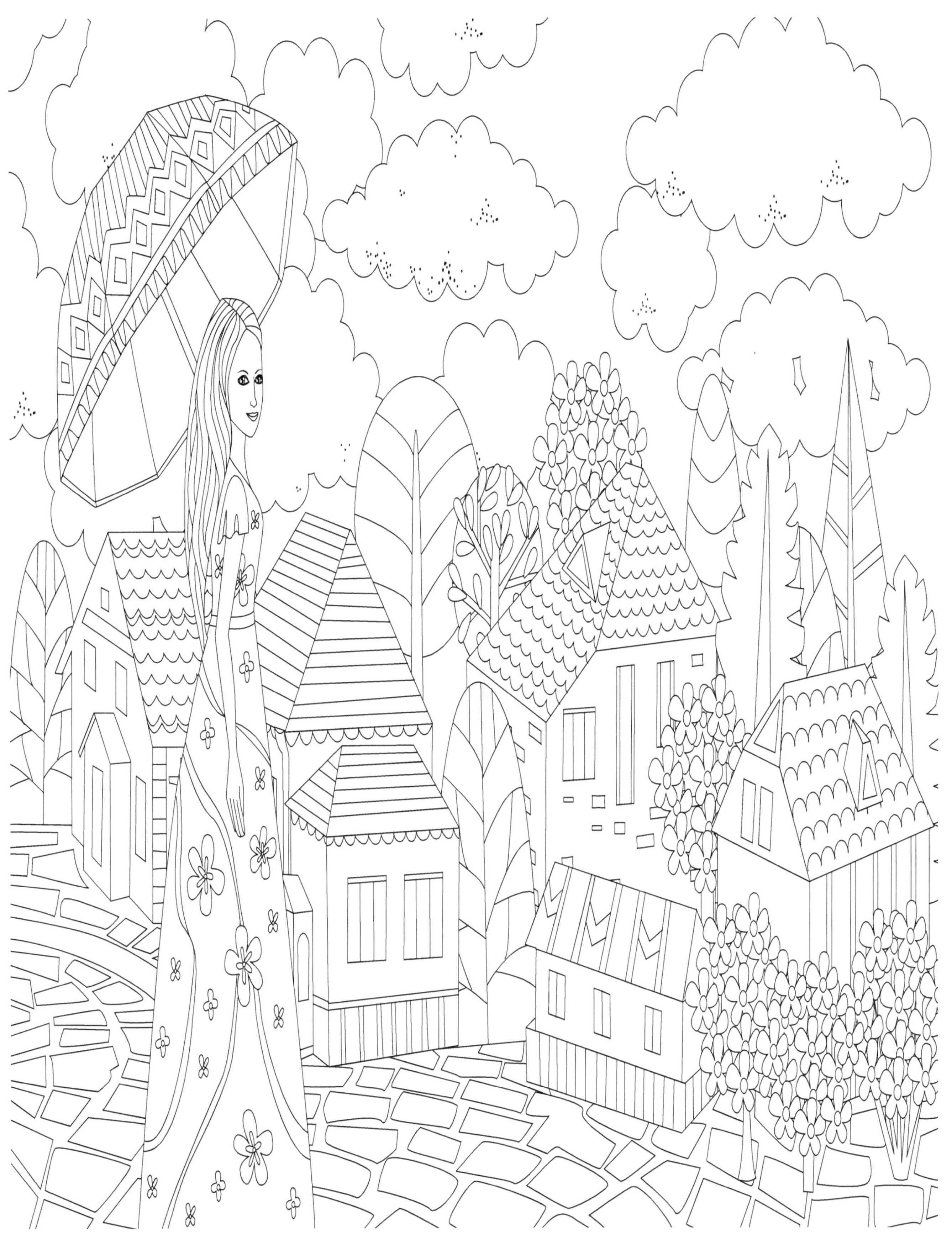

More Coloring Books by HAPPY ARTS COLORING. Available on AMAZON.

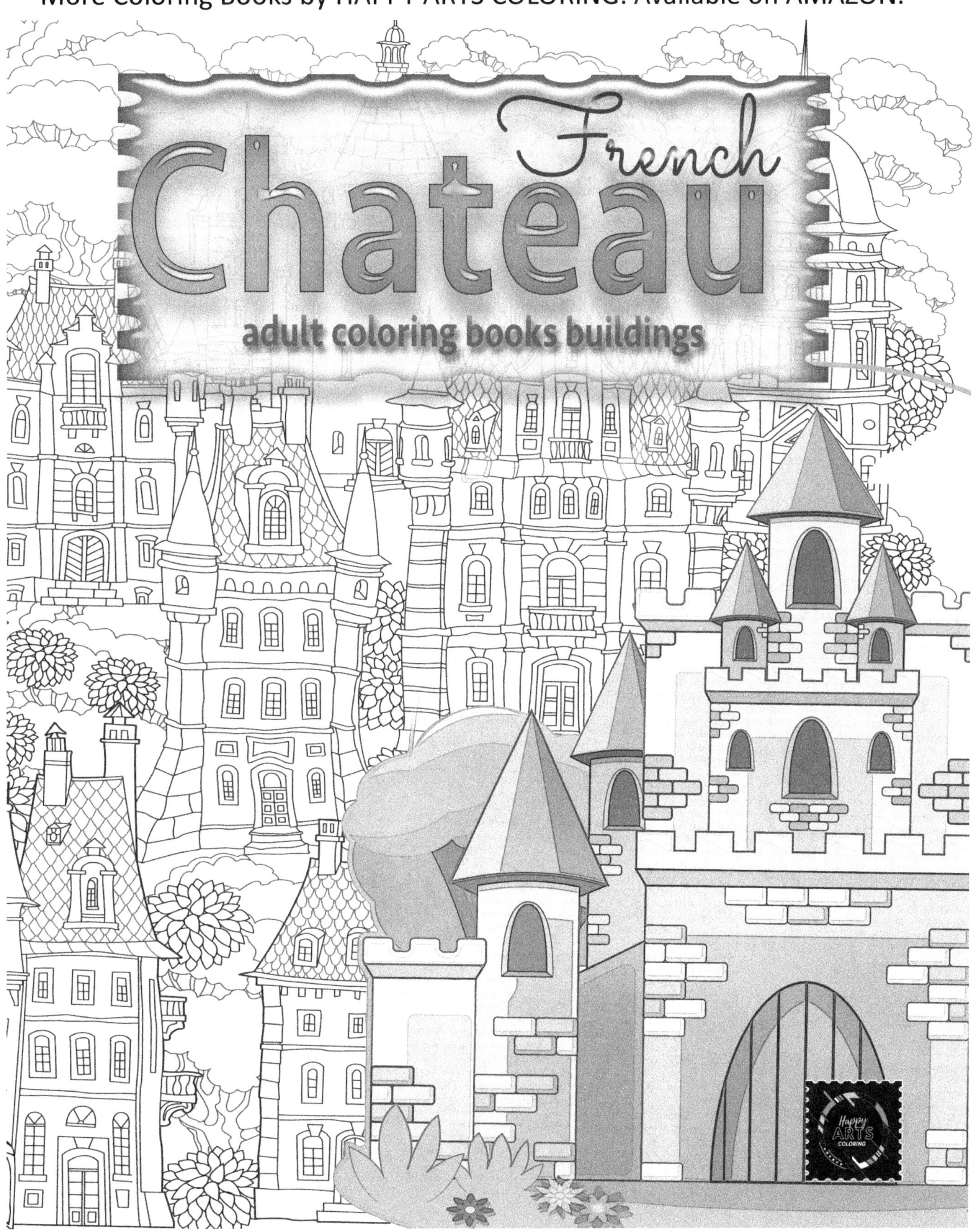

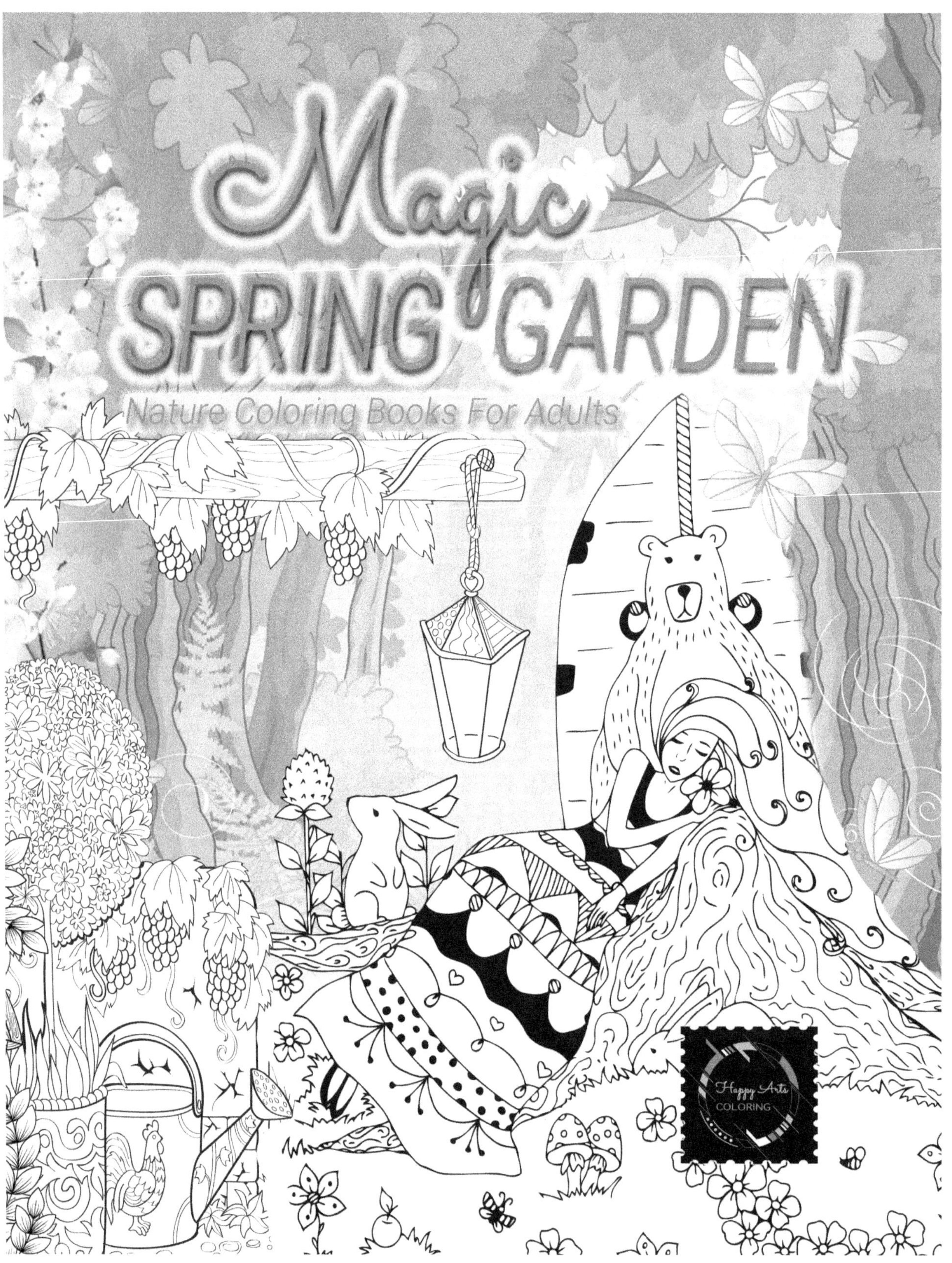

Magic
SPRING GARDEN
Nature Coloring Books For Adults
Happy Arts
COLORING

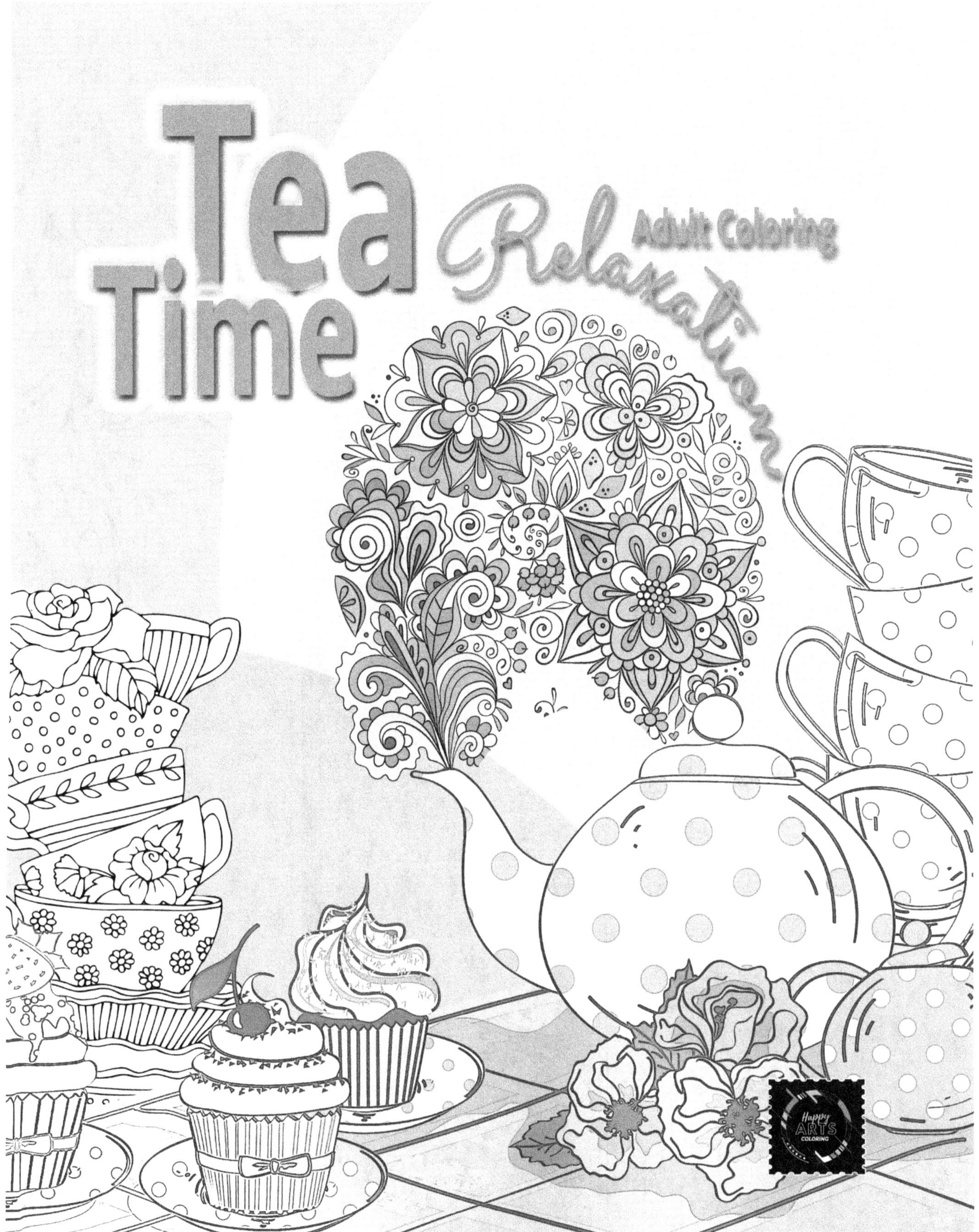

Tea Time
Relaxation
Adult Coloring
Happy ARTS COLORING

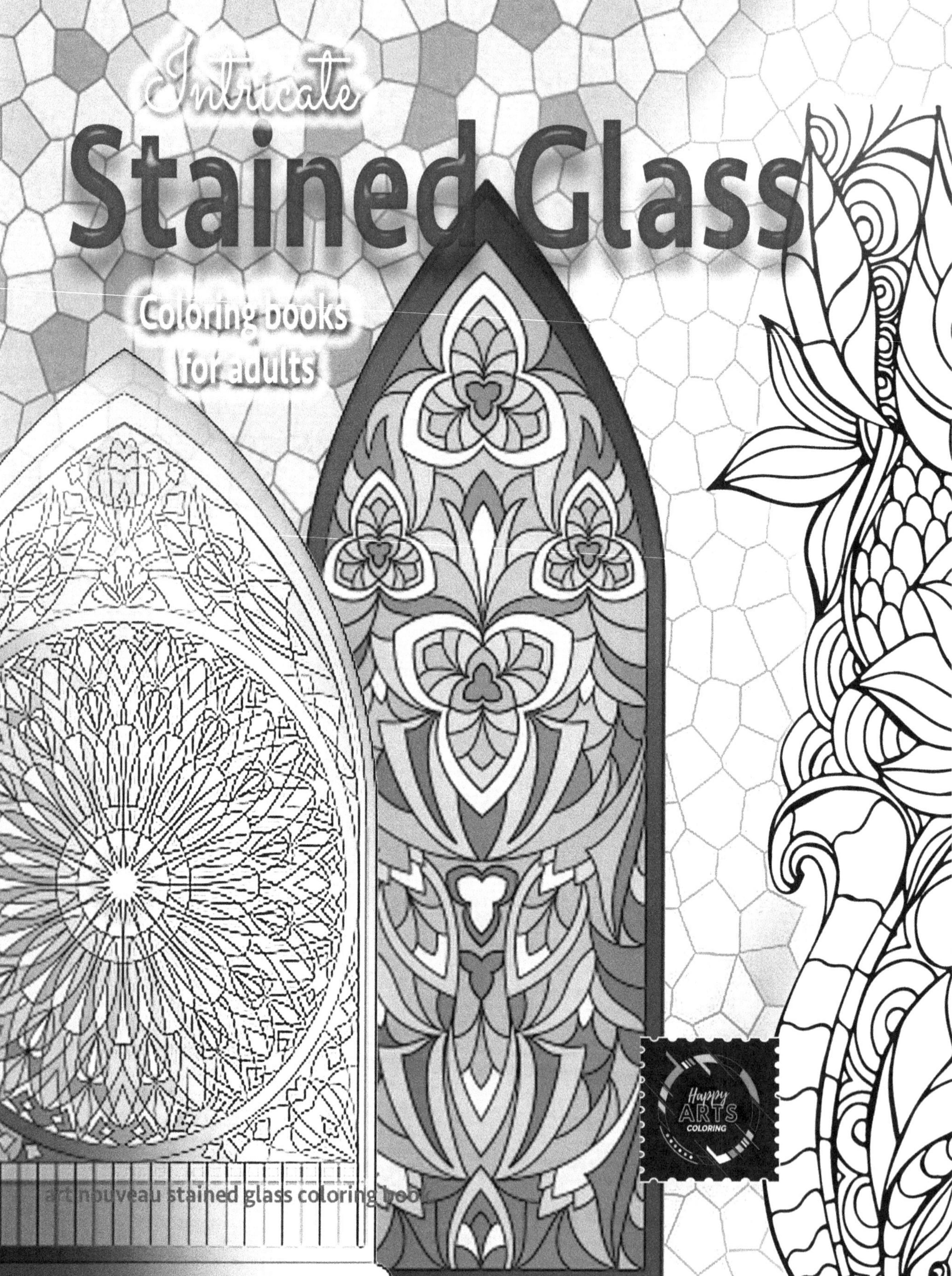

Intricate
Stained Glass
Coloring books
for adults
Happy ARTS COLORING
art nouveau stained glass coloring book

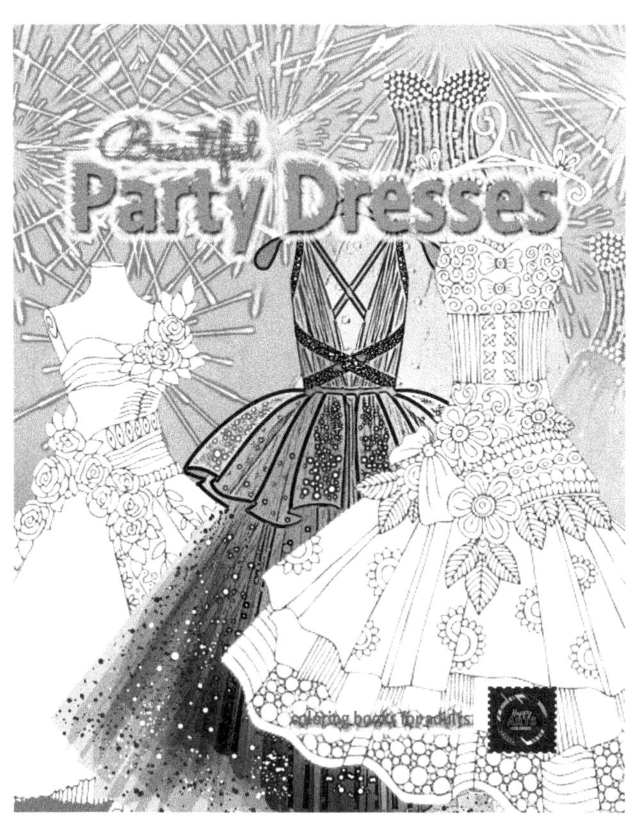

Beautiful
Party Dresses
coloring books for adults

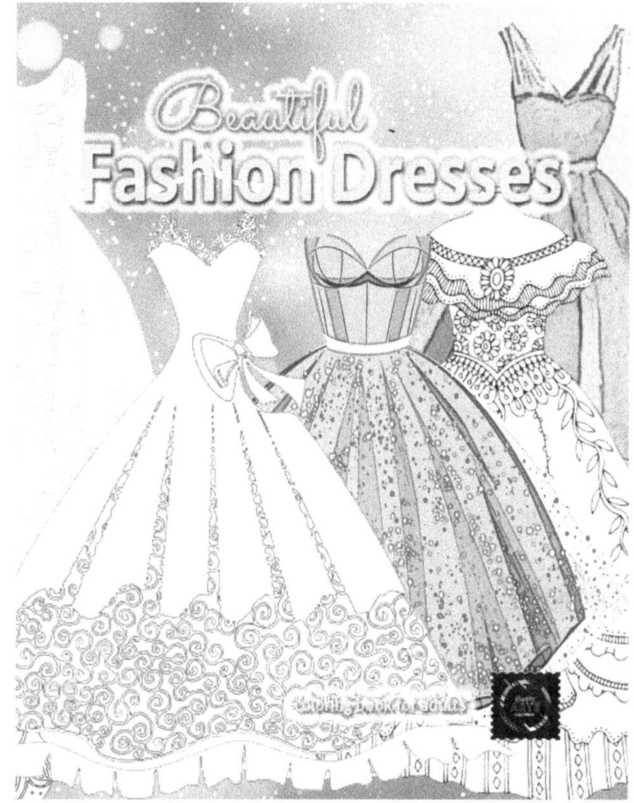

Beautiful
Fashion Dresses
coloring books for adults

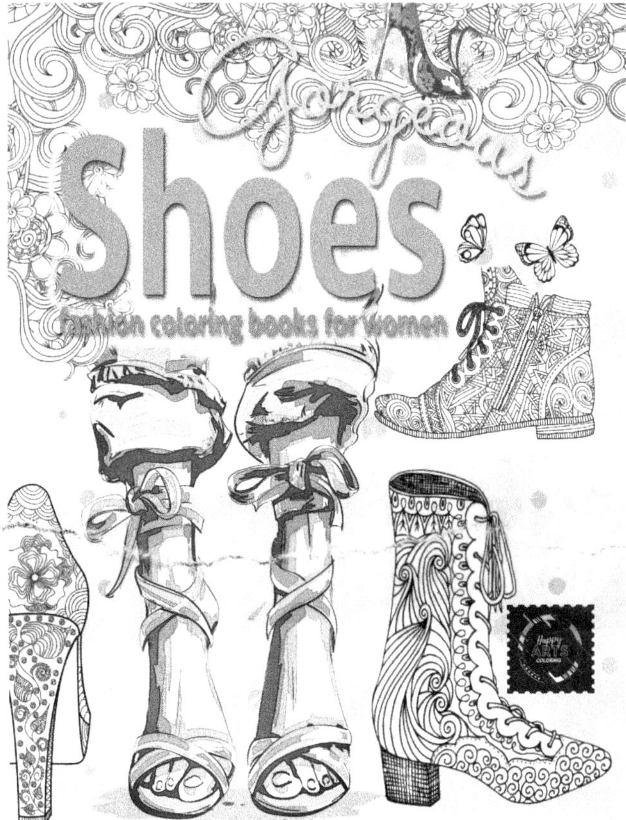

Gorgeous
Shoes
fashion coloring books for women

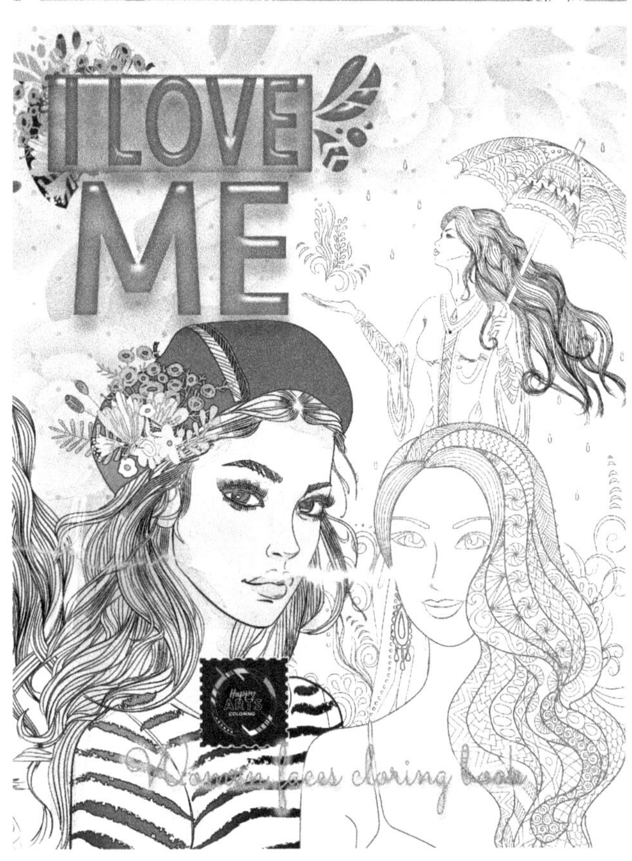

I LOVE
ME
Women faces coloring book

www.ingramcontent.com/pod-product-compliance
Lightning Source LLC
LaVergne TN
LVHW080549200726
843510LV00008B/1061